PLAYING ON THE CHANGES

bob mintzer

MW00803906

CONTENTS

Alfred Music
P.O. Box 10003
Van Nuys, CA 91410-0003
alfred.com

All etudes composed and arranged by BOB MINTZER
© 2015 MINTZER MUSIC CO. (ASCAP)
Exclusive Worldwide Distribution by ALFRED MUSIC
All Rights Reserved. Used by Permission.

ISBN-10: 1-4706-2316-1
ISBN-13: 978-1-4706-2316-6

INTRODUCTION

The idea to write this book came from two separate situations. The first was the experience of teaching aspiring students of improvisation who, in their eagerness to play with intensity and emotion in their solos, had circumvented the ability to play on any chord quality in all twelve keys and also truly tell a story that was melodic, colorful, and moving gracefully through the harmony of the tune. The second situation came from my own quest to practice music that expands my improvising ability to navigate any harmonic setting with a sense of ease, connection, and depth.

The thirteen etudes in this book take you through the various chord qualities found in standards and jazz tunes in such a way that, in each case, you cover all twelve keys. Practicing music that takes me through all the keys helps my ears and enables me to play on changes by relying on feel rather than intellect. I can more easily improvise in a spontaneous and connected way, and my thought process can then take a back seat to focusing on the people I am playing with. When I solo, I try to put together an improvisation with connectivity, shape, momentum, and elements that the listening ear can follow.

Modeled after music I would improvise, these etudes contain a good deal of repetition, sequential lines that move gracefully through the changes, melodic and rhythmic patterns that create continuity, and singable melodies. For me, it's all about the song! I try to find ways to use the colorful notes (9ths, 11ths, 13ths) in strategic ways.

As with my other etude books, I've written out solos that traverse the changes in a way that familiarizes you with the sound of each harmonic setting. Areas covered include major 7th chords, minor 7th chords, dominant 7th chords (Mixolydian, altered, and half-whole diminished), minor ii(♭5) chords, tritone substitutions, and a variety of progressions using all the above. For each chord quality I suggest you initially practice a few things in advance. I break down the practice to four key areas or configurations.

1. Play the corresponding scale from bottom to top on your instrument.

2. Play the scale in 3rds up and down.

3. Play the scale in a variation of 3rds pattern (1, 3, 4, 2; 3, 5, 6, 4; 5, 7, 8, 6).

4. Play the scale in diatonic 7ths (1, 3, 5, 7; 8, 6, 4, 2; 3, 5, 7, 9; 10, 8, 6, 4).

Listen to and analyze the etudes. The real fun begins when you begin to play along with the rhythm section to solo on the etudes; just mute the solo tenor sax in the TNT 2 mixer. If you get to a particular spot in an etude where you are struggling to find something to play, use the software to loop any section on the track and repeat as needed at any tempo. Or better yet, stop and then, over a given chord play the corresponding scale in the four configurations mentioned above. And feel free to slow down the tempo to get those rhythmically challenging passages and "double time" figures under your fingers.

I do hope you enjoy the journey I've set up through the twelve keys and various chord progressions. One thing is for certain. I will be using this book as much as you!

Bob Mintzer

My thanks to the fine musicians on the DVD disk:

Russ Ferrante, piano
Will Kennedy, drums
Paul Henry, bass

Tracks recorded at Bias Studios, Springfield, VA
Engineered by Jim Robison

CUSTOM MIX

1. For installation, insert the DVD into a computer, and double-click on **My Computer**.

2. Right-click on the CD drive icon, and select Explore. (Mac users can simply double-click the DVD icon that appears on the desktop.)

3. Open the "**DVD-ROM** Materials" folder and then the "**TNT 2**" folder.

4. Double-click the installation file. Installation may take up to 15 minutes.

SYSTEM REQUIREMENTS

Windows
7, Vista, XP
1.8 GHz processor or faster
2.1 GB hard drive space, 2 GB RAM minimum
DVD drive for installation
Speakers or headphones
Internet access required for updates

Macintosh
OS 10.4 and higher (Intel only)
2.1 GB hard drive space, 2 GB RAM minimum
DVD drive for installation
Speakers or headphones
Internet access required for updates

BIO

Bob Mintzer is a GRAMMY®-winning saxophonist, composer, arranger, and educator who started in the music scene around 1974. After attending Hart College of Music and Manhattan School of Music, Bob joined the bands of Tito Puente and Eumir Deodato, touring the world and playing regularly around New York City.

Around 1975, Bob joined the Buddy Rich Big Band and spent two-and-a-half years there. On Buddy's band, Bob started writing arrangements and wrote/recorded eight charts. On the road, Buddy and the band played every night of the year with two weeks off at Christmas time.

In 1978, Bob signed on with the Thad Jones Mel Lewis Orchestra, continuing to write and perform and playing with other jazz luminaries, such as Art Blakey, Joe Chambers, Sam Jones, and Tom Harrell, around New York, and dove into the freelance music scene in the city.

From 1981–82, Bob was a member of the Jaco Pastorius Word of Mouth band, making several recordings and touring extensively.

In 1983, Bob started his first big band, recording an album for CBS/Sony called *Papa Lips*. The first band included wonderful players such as Dave Sanborn, Michael and Randy Brecker, Peter Erskine, and Don Grolnick. The band performed regularly at 7th Avenue South and the Village Vanguard during this time. Subsequently the band went on to make 14 CDs for the esteemed DMP label over a 22-year period.

In 1990, Bob joined the Yellowjackets, recording the CD *Greenhouse* and embarking on a venture that is still in progress today. The band travels the world and continues to release innovative and distinctive recordings.

The next milestone was in 2001, when the Bob Mintzer Big Band CD *Homage to Count Basie* won a GRAMMY for Best Large Jazz Ensemble Album. In 2006 Bob joined forces with the Manchester Craftsmen's Guild label, and has made six CDs with MCG to date.

In addition to all this, he has performed and/or written for hundreds of recordings, as well as played with orchestras such as the New York Philharmonic, the Hollywood Bowl Orchestra, the Metropole Orchestra, the National Symphony Orchestra, and the Buffalo Philharmonic Orchestra.

Bob has written over 300 big band arrangements, many of which are still performed throughout the world. He has published several etude books, a piano book, and a solo transcription book for Alfred Music.

Bob is currently on the faculty of the USC Thornton School of Music in the Bowen H. "Buzz" and Barbara M. McCoy Endowed Chair in Jazz position. He and his wife live in the Hollywood Hills in a former home of Arnold Schoenberg.

For more information on Bob, his performances, and writing, please visit bobmintzer.com.

How to use the DVD-ROM with the  Software

1. Listen to the quartet perform the etude you want to study (mute the click track if desired).

2. Analyze the etude scale, chord progression, melody, shape, and rhythmic figures.

3. Practice the etude with no accompaniment with your metronome. Begin at a tempo that is comfortable and increase the tempo as desired.

4. To play along with the trio using the TNT 2 software, mute the saxophone part (mute the click track if desired).

5. To master each etude, you are encouraged to slow down the tempo using the TNT 2 software. Then increase the tempo as you begin to master the etude.

6. Using the TNT 2 software, loop sections to focus on a particular challenging section.

ETUDE 1
dorian mode

The Dorian mode with minor 3rd and minor 7th scale degrees is used on minor 7th chords. Practice the scale up and down at various tempos. Then practice Pattern 1: Thirds; Pattern 2: Variation in Thirds; and Pattern 3: Diatonic Sevenths.

The Dorian Mode

Pattern 1: Thirds

Pattern 2: Variation in Thirds (1, 3, 4, 2)

1 3 4 2 3 5 6 4 5 7 8 6 etc.

Pattern 3: Diatonic Sevenths (1, 3, 5, 7, 8, 6, 4, 2)

After practicing the Dorian scale in these four configurations, you can create some interesting melodic shapes when you play either of the two following pentatonic scales:

Minor Pentatonic with a Minor 7th

Minor Pentatonic with a Major 6th

1 3 4 2 3 5 6 4 etc.

ETUDE 1
dorian mode

C Instruments

This page is left blank to facilitate page turns.

ETUDE 2
major 7th

As in Etude 1, practice the major scale (Ionian mode) up and down, then the major pentatonic scale, and then Patterns 1, 2, and 3.

Major Pentatonic Scale

Pattern 1: Major Pentatonic in Thirds

Pattern 2: Major Pentatonic Scale Variations in Thirds (1, 3, 4, 2)

Pattern 3: Major Pentatonic Scale in Diatonic Sevenths

Playing the major pentatonic scale in these configurations results in several colorful melodies, where color notes (9ths and 13ths) are played on strong beats. You will notice I use melodies based on this pentatonic scale quite a lot in Etude 2. Notice a four eighth-note rhythmical motif throughout the etude. This repetition of the motif holds the piece together. It might also be worth noting how the lines breathe and where they pause. In m. 65 of the etude, I wrote triplet figures in various groupings. This can create an interesting feeling of rhythmic tension for a brief moment. Groupings of four in a triplet feel are a great idea; experiment with this rhythmical pattern!

Four-note Groupings in a Triplet Feel

ETUDE 2
major 7th

C Instruments

ETUDE 3
altered dominant

Now the plot thickens! The altered dominant scale is an extremely colorful and versatile scale. It is generally used over a dominant 7th chord with a raised 5th and a ♯9. The "altered" quality of the scale makes it useful in a V–I situation, where the altered V chord wants to resolve to the I chord. Many colorful notes are in this scale: ♭9, ♯9, ♯11, and ♯5. As with the other scale qualities, it is great to play this exercise in the four configurations. Practice the scale up and down, and Patterns 1, 2, and 3.

The Altered Dominant Scale

Pattern 1: Thirds

Pattern 2: Variation in Thirds (1, 3, 4, 2)

Pattern 3: Diatonic Sevenths

Just about all of this etude is based on one of these scale patterns. I did this intentionally to demonstrate how you can toggle between the four patterns in a way that winds up sounding more melodic than pattern-like. After all, the idea here is to be able to improvise melodies, not patterns. Practicing the patterns is a good way to get the sound in your ears. The next step is to configure your melodies in a less predictable way. Rhythmical phrasing helps with this. Rather than playing a constant stream of eighth notes, I play shorter phrases with some level of repetition and connection between the phrases. Below is a good example of a nice melodic and rhythmical phrase in Etude 3, mm. 37–40.

A Melodic and Rhythmical Phrase

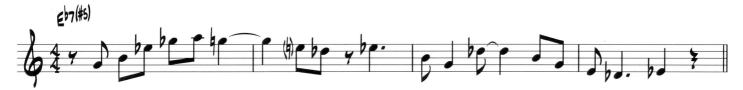

ETUDE 3
altered dominant

C INSTRUMENTS

ETUDE 4
half-whole diminished

The half-whole diminished scale is the twin brother of the altered dominant scale. It can be used on dominant 7th chords or 13th chords with a natural 6th or 13th degree rather than the altered or raised 5th. It works on a I or V dominant 7th chord because the major 6th does not tend to resolve. This scale has ♭9, ♯9, and ♯11 degrees. Hence it can be played to color a straight dominant 7th chord, or over a 13th(♭9♯11) chord. Practice the scale and Patterns 1, 2, and 3.

Half-Whole Diminished Scale

Pattern 1: Thirds

Pattern 2: Variation in Thirds (1, 3, 4, 2)

Pattern 3: Diatonic Sevenths (Note that each four-note grouping is a diminished 7th chord!)

In this etude I tried to get away from the predictability of patterns by using large interval jumps, triads that are built into the scale, and rhythms (like 3 against 4) that break up the four-note pattern. Leaving space at the end of phrases can also make lines sound more melodic. In m. 13 and m. 14 in the etude, you will notice four triads that are outlined from this scale. Observe that over the C13(♭9♯11) chord, the C, E♭, G♭, and A triads are outlined.

Four-triad Concept

Experiment with this four-triad concept, and discover some very interesting things to play!

ETUDE 4
half-whole diminished

C Instruments

ETUDE 5
minor 7th chords a minor third apart

This is a great chord exercise to practice playing melodically and horizontally (rather than up and down the chords) through a series of minor 7th chords. The etude is structured in such a way that you wind through all 12 keys. I threw in an altered dominant chord at the end of each eight-measure phrase to move you to the next series of minor 7th chords. One way to organize soloing on this progression would be to play the same chord tone on the downbeat for each chord. Try one pass playing the minor 3rd on each chord on the downbeat, and then try the 5th or minor 7th, 9th, or 11th.

9th on Downbeat

You will notice that on several occasions in a four-measure phrase, I repeat a rhythmical and melodic motif three times and then finish up the phrase with a "wind-up." This is a great thing to practice doing in your soloing. It will add a compositional element to your playing, take some of the randomness out of what you play, and give the listener something to grab onto! I sometimes use the analogy of how one might tell a friend what a day was like in four short connected phrases: "I woke up, got dressed, went to school, and had a pretty good day!" The pattern example above demonstrates this concept. You'll notice the etudes begin to get into some more involved rhythmical territory. I'm using 4 against 3 triplet figures as well as double-time sixteenth-note lines. With the TNT 2 software, you're able to slow down the etude to play along. Find a tempo that is comfortable for you. Try not to get discouraged if you can't play some of this up to tempo right away. Believe me, I couldn't play all of this up to tempo without practicing! Take a look at mm. 53–54 and mm. 61–62 from the etude. Below are two examples of playing a triplet pulse in groupings of four. This is a fertile rhythmical area for any kind of improvising, and should be practiced as a stand-alone entity.

Four-note Groupings with a Triplet Pulse

Notice how I began the Fmi7 phrase on the minor 3rd, and then the D minor 7th line on the 5th, so as to create a graceful and melodic route through the harmony. I sometimes tell my students, "We want to play melodies, not chords, in our solos." Of course, the melodies we choose should reflect the harmony in an interesting way, but that should not be the primary purpose.

Both of these phrases below begin on the sus4 of the chord. Colorful!

Beginning on the Suspended 4th

ETUDE 5
minor 7th chords a minor third apart

ETUDE 6
major 7th chords a minor third apart

This etude is similar to Etude 5. What I wrote in this etude is the end result of becoming comfortable with the movement of major 7th chords in this way. The phrasing has a good deal of rhythmical repetition, and I tried to find common tones between the chords wherever possible, or at the very least, tried to move stepwise and gracefully between the chords.

Below are a few examples of an ostinato figure you could play through these chord changes to become more familiar with the sound of these phrases.

Ostinato Figures

In this example above, I am outlining arpeggios that include lots of color, specifically the major 7th, 9th, and 13th. There is something about the way this sounds that I really like. I used this sound quite a bit in this etude. Try to add some scalular motion in between the arpeggios to have some variety in the line, and to also connect the chords together in a musical way.

Measures 73–76 in the etude provide a clear example of playing the major pentatonic scale, or close to it, in thirds. I do this for each chord over two measures. Again, observe the rhythmical and motivic repetition. Use these ideas in your improvisation!

Major Pentatonic Scale in Thirds

ETUDE 6
major 7th chords a minor third apart

ETUDE 7
ii–V–I–VI minor thirds apart

The ii–V–I–VI progression is the backbone of traditional jazz music and well beyond just jazz. The process of taking this progression through all 12 keys is one of the best vocabulary and ear-training builders I know. The etude begins with a lick or quote you may recognize, certainly one of the hippest ii–V–I melodies and chord progressions.

Beginning ii–V–I Melody and Chord Progression

One of the best things about this melody is that it starts on the chord's sus4, which offers a very colorful sound and ends up on the 13th, also colorful. Also, the large sixth interval is surrounded by two smaller intervals. This combination of a large interval and smaller intervals around it is a characteristic of many great melodies, including "Over the Rainbow," "Invitation," and "I Love You," to name a few.

A nice challenge is to play this familiar lick for every ii–V–I in this etude. It's not written out, so doing this will also sharpen your ear and add a compositional slant to your improvising. There is a nice opportunity to get your altered dominant melodies in on the VI chords of these progessions. You will observe in this etude that I'm accessing the altered dominant pretty heavily in each instance.

The goal is to 1) familiarize your ear with the sound and feel of the ii–V–I–VI progression in all keys, and 2) be able to "spin a tale," i.e., play something melodic where there is a logical connection between phrases—a flow where one phrase takes the listening ear to the next phrase. This is accomplished through repetition, framing your phrases with silence, and constructing melodies that are a combination of elements so as to not sound like an exercise. Use this concept—it works! Hint: Classic standards and tunes such as "Honeysuckle Rose" are jam-packed with melodies that will enrich your ability to improvise on these kinds of progressions with a high level of musicality. Isolate any of the lines in this etude, and play them in all 12 keys!

When you improvise, practice taking a short rhythmical motif and play it through the whole etude, as in this example below.

Short Rhythmic Motifs from Etude 7

ETUDE 7
ii–V–I–VI minor thirds apart

C INSTRUMENTS

This page is left blank to facilitate page turns.

ETUDE 8
dominant 7th chords in cycle of fourths

This etude is all about the bebop language. I've incorporated the various chromatic motions that are common to this bebop style of playing. One of the chromatic devices I use is sometimes referred to as the "enclosure." The enclosure is when the note is preceded by a half step above and a half step below a chord tone. In m. 1 on beat 4, I enclose the 3rd of the chord in the second measure.

The Enclosure

The main focus in this etude is rhythmical phrasing. I tried to connect the phrases together in a call-and-response fashion, where one phrase leads logically to the next. Try to play the rhythms in the etude, and then add your own notes as a side exercise.

Check out this etude, where the triplet figures begin in m. 25. Then in m. 27, I employ groupings of four triplet-eighth notes. Take it a few times through to get comfortable with this rhythm. To me, it's a nice way of creating rhythmical interest.

Sixteenth-note lines are interspersed throughout this etude. Practice them by slowing down the tempo with the TNT 2 software before trying to play them at the suggested tempo. They are fairly diatonic as is the whole etude, so hopefully it should not be too challenging. When playing sixteenth-note lines, try to play light and *legato*, accenting occasional notes in the bebop fashion. Don't play loud! The tendency with a technically demanding passage is to play loud, but the key is to play light and on top of the time!

In mm. 57–60 in this etude, I wrote lines that moved scalularly through from one chord to the next, as shown below. I believe this is a logicial way to practice moving through a set of chord changes.

Play the corresponding scale for the first chord, then move stepwise to the first note in the next chord, and then adjust the scale to conform to that harmony.

Scalular Motion

ETUDE 8
dominant 7th chords in cycle of fourths

C Instruments

Shuffle ♩ = 124
(Flute optional 8va)

37

ETUDE 9
minor ii7(♭5)–V

The minor 7(♭5)–V–I or ii7(♭5)–V–I progression is another harmonic scenario you will frequently encounter when soloing in jazz. The minor 7th(♭5) scale is generally the Locrian mode of the chord with a natural 2nd scale degree. You could also think of it as a melodic minor scale a minor 3rd above the chord root. For example, for Gmi7(♭5), play the B♭ melodic minor scale.

Melodic Minor Scale a Minor 3rd Above the Root

Be sure to practice this scale in the four configurations: the scale up and down, in thirds, in variations of thirds, and in diatonic sevenths. The diatonic seventh configuration below sounds particularly interesting.

Scale in Diatonic Sevenths

Examine the first two measures of note choices in the example below. The first note on a strong beat is the 9th of the Gmi7(♭5) chord. This is a colorful note. The second note, F♯, is the major 7th of G and functions as a passing note or chromatic approach from below the next note, G. Again, the major 7th adds color and some level of complexity that sounds good when you resolve to the root. It could also be thought of as a Gmi/maj7th sound. The last note in the first measure (E♭) is tied to the downbeat of the second measure, and is the ♯9 of the C7 chord—again, another color note that sounds great. I wrote this with the ♯9, then with a ♭9 (D♭), followed by a large interval skip down to the 3rd of the C7 chord.

9ths and Major 7ths

Measures 59 and 60 from this etude demonstrate groupings of four in triplets. This is then followed by sixteenth notes. Notice how I try to lead gracefully up to the sixteenth-note passages, starting with sparse eighth-note lines, following with triplets, and then moving on to a short flurry of sixteenth notes. When I improvise, I always try to think with rhythmical variety.

Finally, the last two measures have a grouping of six eighth-note patterns that could be used in a multitude of settings. Don't be afraid to take one or more measures and play the shape in other settings.

Eighth-note Patterns

ETUDE 9
minor ii7(♭5)–V

C Instruments

ETUDE 10
minor 7th chords up 2, down 1

Here's another progression that will expand your ears to interpret the chord changes. The idea is to move in a melodic way that doesn't obviously outline the chords. Moving scalewise from one measure to the next can achieve this. In this etude, mm. 1–2 and mm. 4–5 clearly do this. The goal is for the scalular motion to sound melodic rather than chordal. As in the other etudes, my compositions frequently land on 9ths on strong beats. Three of the first five measures utilize this concept, as demonstrated in the example below.

Melodic Scalular Motion

As shown in the example below, mm. 41–44 from this etude have a repeating three eighth-note grouping format, which adds a level of rhythmical interest and continuity through repetition. These four measures are loaded with 9ths, 11ths, and 13ths. The goal is to combine colorful note choices with a rhythmical pattern that creates some level of intrigue—a win-win situation! As with the other etudes, play through this example and discover what the phrases look and sound like, and how one moves to the next. You will find quite a bit of repetition and sequential motion. Take one or more of these examples, and try to utilize it elsewhere in your improvisation. Create!

Eighth-note Groupings of Three

Finally, look at mm. 65–67 from this etude in the example below. I repeated a rhythmical figure where there is an emphasized note on beat 4 tied to the next measure. The notes on beat 4 anticipate the harmony of the next measure. I think this is a creative way to establish some tension and resolution while creating continuity with a repeating rhythmical motif.

Emphasized Beat 4

ETUDE 10
minor 7th chords up 2, down 1

44

ETUDE 11
major 7th chords down 2, up 1

Similar structural principles apply in this etude, as in Etude 10. Practice moving scalularly through the changes, find common tones, and settle on rhythmical motifs to repeat through the changes. Remember the concept of "Got up, got dressed, did my errands, and went out to see what the day would bring." Three short phrases with a wind-up, or a fourth phrase that is longer and wraps up the idea.

This etude begins with a quarter-note, two eighth-note, quarter-note motif. It can be found in the first, second, fourth, sixth, and ninth measures. Some of these motifs are anticipated with an eighth note tied from the prior measure. I try to elaborate with each consecutive statement of the motif to create some variety and forward motion, as in the example below.

Beginning Motif

Etude 11 is a good choice to practice playing the major 7th of each chord on the downbeat of the measure, as I demonstrated in the example above. Next, try playing the 9th of each chord on the downbeat of each measure. Then play the major 3rd on each downbeat. This activity will sharpen your ears and help to add compositional thinking to your improvising.

Observe mm. 65–67 from the etude in the example below. Here is another example of a repeated rhythmical motif that incorporates using specific intervals throughout. You will see a series of fifth and fourth intervals that ascend in each measure. This is another example of a compositional device that can be practiced to eventually use when soloing. Try the same thing with third, sixth, and even seventh intervals. The more varying devices of this kind you can get under your belt, the more interesting and compositional your solos will be, I promise!

Ascending Fourths and Fifths

ETUDE 11
major 7th chords down 2, up 1

ETUDE 12
tritone subs

The tritone substitution is another way of using an altered dominant sound on the V chord in a ii–V progression. It is one of the most colorful ways to approach the ii–V–I progression. Essentially, you are plugging in a ii–V a tritone away from the tonic ii–V, in place of the tonic V chord. Below is an example using a snippet from the melody of a familiar standard tune. Practice this in all 12 keys!

Tritone Substitution

Another way to look at it is to think melodic minor a half-step above the V chord—the altered scale. Therefore, A♭ melodic minor and a G7 altered scale are one and the same! Check out the example below.

G7alt = A♭ Melodic Minor Scale

So, as you can see in the above example, there is a direct correlation between G7alt and A♭mi7, as well as G7 and D♭7. The interesting stuff happens when you play the new ii–V diatonically. In the melodic snippet above, observe that over the A♭mi7–D♭7 chord, there is a G♭. This is the major 7th of G, which you would not normally play on a dominant 7th chord. However, in this instance, it goes by as a momentary dissonance and sounds interesting. The other notes in this phrase wind up being the ♭5, ♯5, and ♯9, all colorful notes! The other reason tritone subs sound so interesting is that you are creating a parallel melodic zone that alternately complements and rubs against the diatonic harmony. All the bebop cats used this technique, and, ultimately, John Coltrane used a similar technique with his "Giant Steps" changes—a chord progression that he could superimpose over other progressions or over a single chord vamp.

One last interesting connection in this tritone business is the fact that the altered dominant scale winds up being the Mixolydian ♯4 of the dominant 7th chord a tritone away.

Mixolydian (♯4) Scale

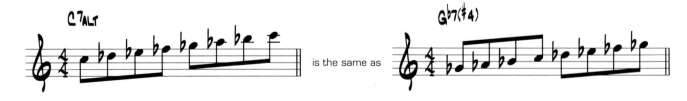

is the same as

ETUDE 12
tritone subs

C Instruments

ETUDE 13
dorian with changes on the end

Etude 13 will give you a shot at the minor Dorian mode in all 12 keys with a descending ii–V progression on the end of each 12-measure section. This etude is based on a pentatonic scale that includes the major 6th in a variety of configurations. Play the scale below up and down at various tempos and then Patterns 1 and 2.

Minor Pentatonic with a Major 6th

Pattern 1: Thirds

Pattern 2: Variations (1, 3, 4, 2, 3, 5, 6, 4)

When playing on one chord for eight measures or more, you can do many different things to elaborate on the diatonic harmony of that one chord. You might even think of the root of the chord as a pedal note, where you can play virtually anything against it, with notes not in the quality of the chord. Let's begin with possibilities within the diatonic harmony of the music. You can always refer to the V chord in your improvising by superimposing a I–V–I line into your solo. Observe mm. 13–15 from the etude in the example below. Play on eight measures of concert B♭mi7. In m. 14, I outline an F7alt chord and then return to B♭mi7 on the "and" of beat 4 in that measure. You could also think of the F7alt as a B♭mi7.

Solo over I–V–I

Now let's look at an example in which I depart from the diatonic harmony. This example is from mm. 50–53 in the etude. The I–IV–V configuration I play moves up in whole steps, thus creating a parallel, nonspecific harmonic setting. I resolve this in the third measure, where I touch upon Emi–B7(♯5)–Emi.

I–IV–V Moving in Whole Steps

You can move the I–IV–V shape around in different ways. The example below is a I–IV–V ascending a minor third at a time. Challenge yourself, be creative, and think outside the box!

I–IV–V Ascending in Minor 3rds

ETUDE 13
dorian with changes on the end

C Instruments

MEDIUM SWING ♩ = 152
(FLUTE OPTIONAL 8VA)

BOB MINTZER SELECTED DISCOGRAPHY

As Leader

1980 *Horn Man* (CBS/Sony Records)
1981 *Source* (Explore Records)
1984 *Papa Lips* (Explore Records)
1985 *Incredible Journey* (DMP)
1985 *The First Decade* (compilation) (DMP)
1986 *Camouflage* (DMP)
1988 *Spectrum* (DMP)
1989 *Urban Contours* (DMP)
1990 *Hymn* (OWL)
1990 *The Art of the Big Band* (DMP)
1991 *I Remember Jaco* (Jive/Novus)
1991 *One Music* (DMP)
1991 *Departure* (DMP)
1993 *Only in New York* (DMP)
1994 *Twin Tenors* (Novus)
1995 *Big Band Trane* (DMP)
1996 *Live at Jazz Club Fasching* (Dragon)
1998 *Latin from Manhattan* (DMP)
1998 *Quality Time* (TVT)
2000 *Homage to Count Basie* (DMP) (GRAMMY®)
2003 *Gently* (DMP)
2004 *Live at MCG* (MCG Jazz)
2005 *In the Moment* (Art of Life Records)
2006 *Old School New Lessons* (MCG Jazz)
2008 *Swing Out* (MCG Jazz)
2009 *The Music of Bob Mintzer with University of Kentucky* (Mark Records)
2009 *Spirit of Iceland* with Reykjavic Big Band
2010 *Canyon Cove* (Pony Canyon Records)
2012 *For the Moment* (MCG Jazz)
2014 *R&B Big Band* (MCG Jazz)

With the Yellowjackets

1990 *Greenhouse* (GRP)
1992 *Live Wires* (GRP)
1992 *Like a River* (GRP)
1993 *Run for Your Life* (GRP)
1994 *Dreamland* (Warner Bros.)
1995 *Blue Hats* (Warner Bros.)
1997 *Club Nocturne* (Warner Bros.)
2000 *Mint Jam* (Universal/Polygram)
2002 *Time Squared* (Heads Up Records)
2004 *Altered State* (Heads Up Records)
2006 *Twenty-Five* (Heads Up Records)
2008 *Lifecycle* (Heads Up Records)
2010 *Timeline* (Mack Avenue Records)
2012 *A Rise in the Road* (Mack Avenue Records)

As Sideman

1973 Buddy Rich: *Ease on Down the Road* (Laserlight)
1979 Sam Jones: *Something New* (Pony Canyon Records)
1977 Buddy Rich: *No Jive* (Novus)
1980 Buddy Rich: *Live at Ronnie Scott's* (DRG)
1980 Mel Lewis: *Live at the Village Vanguard* (DCC Jazz)
1981 Jaco Pastorius: *The Birthday Concert* (Warner Bros.)
1982 Peter Erskine: *Peter Erskine* (Contemporary/OJC)
1985 Bobby McFerrin: *The Best of Bobby McFerrin*
1986 Steve Winwood: *Back in the High Life* (Island)
1987 Marianne Faithfull: *Strange Weather* (Island)
1988 Peter Erskine: *Motion Poet* (Denon Records)
1988 Lyle Mays: *Street Dreams* (Geffen)
1990 Don Grolnick: *Weaver of Dreams* (Blue Note)
1990 Randy Brecker: *Toe to Toe* (MCA Jazz)
1992 Peter Erskine: *Sweet Soul* (Fuzzy Records)
1991 George Gruntz: *Blues 'n Dues Et Cetera* (Enja)
1991 James Taylor: *New Moon Shine* (Columbia)
1992 Special EFX: *Global Village* (GRP)
1992 GRP All-Star Big Band: *GRP All-Star Big Band* (GRP)
1996 GRP All-Star Big Band: *GRP All-Star Big Band* (Video) (GRP)
1993 Michael Franks: *Dragonfly Summer* (Reprise/Warner Bros.)
1993 GRP All-Star Big Band: *GRP All-Star Big Band: Live!* (GRP)
1994 GRP All-Star Big Band: *All Blues* (GRW)
1995 Bobby McFerrin: *Bang! Zoom* (Blue Note)
1995 Steve Winwood: *The Finer Things* (Island)
1995 Michael Franks: *Abandoned Garden* (Warner Bros.)
1998 Marilyn Scott: *Avenues of Love* (Warner Bros.)
1998 Nnenna Freelon: *Maiden Voyage* (Concord Jazz)
2006 Nancy Wilson: *Turned to Blue* (Telarc)
2007 Kurt Elling: *Nightmoves* (Concord Jazz)
2009 Dado Moroni: *Life Is Beautiful* (Abeat)
2010 Fahir Atakoglu: *Faces & Places* (Far&Here LLC)
2010 Billy Cobham: *Drum-n-Voice, Vol. 3* (Neo Membran)
2011 Peter Erskine, Alan Pasqua, Darek Oles, and Bob Mintzer: *Standards 2, Movie Music* (Fuzzy Music)
2012 Arturo Sandoval: *Dear Diz (Every Day I Think of You)* (Concord Jazz)
2014 Mitch Haupers: *Invisible Cities: Original Jazz & Chamber Music* (Liquid Harmony Music)